United States Presidents

James Madison

Anne Welsbacher

ABDO Publishing Company

visit us at
www.abdopub.com

Published by Abdo Publishing Company 4940 Viking Drive, Edina, Minnesota 55435.
Copyright © 1999 by Abdo Consulting Group, Inc. International copyrights reserved in
all countries. No part of this book may be reproduced in any form without written
permission from the publisher.

Published 1999
Printed in the United States of America
Second Printing 2002

Cover and Interior Photo credits: Peter Arnold, Inc., SuperStock, Archive, Corbis-
Bettmann

Edited by Lori Kinstad Pupeza
Contributing editor: Brooke Henderson

Library of Congress Cataloging-in-Publication Data

Welsbacher, Anne, 1955-
    James Madison / Anne Welsbacher.
    p. cm. -- (United States presidents [Edina, Minn.])
    Includes index.
    ISBN 1-56239-739-7
    1. Madison, James, 1751-1836--Juvenile literature. 2. Presidents--United States
    --Biography--Juvenile literature. I. Title. II. Series.
    E342.W45 1998
    973.5'1'092--dc21
    [B]   97-48571
                                             CIP
                                           AC

Revised Edition 2002

Contents

Father of the Constitution

*J*ames Madison was the fourth president of the United States. He is called the Father of the **Constitution**. He was very smart, and planned every part of this important document.

James Madison was an important leader under U.S. President Thomas Jefferson. He helped Jefferson in many ways. Later, James Madison was president of the country during a terrible war, the War of 1812.

As a boy, James Madison was often sick. He loved to read and studied many books all his life. He went to college and finished in only two years!

After college, James Madison began working to help his home colony, Virginia. He soon met Thomas Jefferson, another important Virginia leader. They became lifelong friends.

Opposite page: James Madison, fourth president of the United States

James Madison was one of the strongest leaders of the new United States after it won freedom from England. He helped plan new ideas about how to run the new government. He also developed systems for making and sharing money to support the government. Although they weren't used at the time, his ideas were used later.

James Madison studied many books about the histories of other governments. He used what he learned to help plan the U.S. **Constitution**. This paper explained how the U.S. government would run.

Soon James Madison became one of the leaders in this new government. He helped plan the Bill of Rights. It listed the rights that every American should have.

James Madison and his friend Thomas Jefferson became leaders of a group called the Republicans. They argued with leaders of another group called the Federalists.

James Madison met and soon married Dolley Payne Todd. She was a widow with a son. She was very friendly, and everybody liked her.

James Madison was elected president of the United States. Later, the U.S. was at war with England. English soldiers burned down almost everything in the capital city of Washington, D.C.

James Madison was president for two terms. Then he and Dolley **retired** to Virginia. James Madison died June 28, 1836.

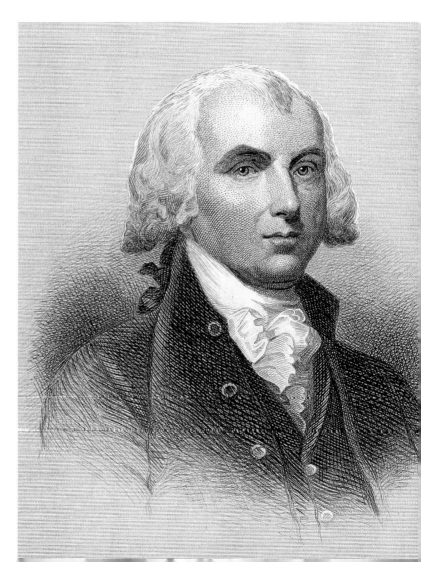

Portrait of James Madison

James Madison (1751-1836)
Fourth President

BORN:	March 16, 1751
PLACE OF BIRTH:	Port Conway, Virginia
ANCESTRY:	English
FATHER:	James Madison (1723-1801)
MOTHER:	Eleanor Conway Madison (1731-1829)
WIFE:	Dorothea (Dolley) Payne Todd (1768-1849)
CHILDREN:	None
EDUCATION:	Early education at Donald Robertson's School and from private tutor; awarded A.B. (1771) from College of New Jersey (Princeton); one year postgraduate study
RELIGION:	Episcopalian
OCCUPATION:	Farmer, lawyer, author
MILITARY SERVICE:	None
POLITICAL PARTY:	Democratic-Republican

OFFICES HELD: Member of Orange County Committee of Safety;
                       Delegate to Virginia Convention; Member of Virginia
                       Legislature; Member of Virginia Executive Council;
                       Delegate to Continental Congress; Delegate to
                       Annapolis Convention; Delegate to Constitutional
                       Convention; Member of Virginia Ratification
                       Convention; U.S. Congressman; Secretary of State

AGE AT INAUGURATION: 57

TERMS SERVED: Two (1809-1813) (1813-1817)

VICE PRESIDENT: George Clinton (1809-1812, died in office) and
                       Elbridge Gerry (1813-1814, died in office)

DIED: June 28, 1836, Montpelier, Virginia, age 85

CAUSE OF DEATH: Natural causes

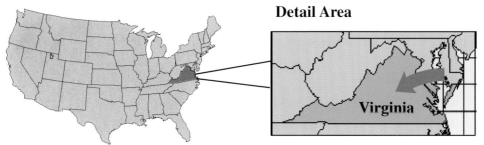

Detail Area

Port Conway,
Virginia

Birthplace of James Madison

Early Years

*J*ames Madison was born in Port Conway, Virginia, on March 16, 1751. Virginia was one of many colonies in America owned by England. The people living in the colonies did not know much about the land west of Virginia.

James was the oldest of 12 children, but five of his siblings died very young. He was shy, with a soft voice. He loved to read. His grandmother taught him lessons, and by the time he was 11, James had read every book in his father's house!

In 1761, when James was nine, his family moved to a new house. They called it Montpelier. It was on a plantation, or big farm, and many slaves farmed the land. James liked to explore the land, look at the Virginia mountains, and wonder what was beyond them.

James was sick often and had **seizures**. He had a disease like epilepsy. James called it a "falling down" disease because when he had a seizure he fell to the floor.

When James was 11 he went away to school. He read books on science, nature, the stars, math, history, and other subjects. He learned about many countries and languages. He liked to ask questions and he read all the time.

At 16, James returned home and studied with a **tutor**. When James was 18, he was ready for college.

Montpelier, in Virginia, was the home of President James Madison.

College Years

Most boys from Virginia went to the College of William and Mary in their home colony in the South. But James went to the College of New Jersey, now called Princeton, in the North. Here he saw many kinds of people and learned new ideas.

The students talked about many things along with their studies. Many people were getting angry. England was charging higher prices on supplies the colonists needed. Yet the colonists were not allowed to raise prices on the supplies they sold to England.

England also charged extra fees called **taxes**. The colonists started talking about breaking away from England and forming the United States. James and other students talked about these things, too.

In class work, James and his best friend Joe Ross studied very hard. College takes four years to finish. But James and Joe finished in only two!

In 1771, James graduated. In 1772, he went home, but he was sad. He was sick, and he did not enjoy his life. His best friend Joe died, and this made him even more sad.

In 1773, the colonists were so angry at England that they threw all the tea it had sent into Boston Harbor! This was called the Boston Tea Party. James was excited. He knew he wanted to be a part of this growing struggle. He decided to get into **politics.**

James Madison

A Virginia Leader

*I*n 1774, James bought some of his father's land. Later that year he was elected to a group to make sure people were prepared to fight England. Now, at age 23, he had his first job in public office, helping his country!

By 1776, the colonies were ready to break free from England. A group called the Second Continental **Congress** wrote an important paper called the **Declaration of Independence**. The paper said the colonies were now a new country, the United States of America.

The Revolutionary War ensured that America was independent. Next, the colonies needed separate states. James Madison joined a group to turn Virginia into a state. He helped the group write an important paper called the Virginia **Constitution** and the Virginia Bill of Rights. The laws and ideas in this paper werc so strong that other colonies used the Virginia Constitution as a model for their own constitutions!

Later, James joined another group of Virginia lawmakers. Here he met an important U.S. leader, Thomas Jefferson. They became lifelong friends.

James believed strongly that people should worship however they wanted. This is called freedom of religion. He worked hard to get this idea into Virginia's law.

This is one of the most important things James Madison did for his country. Today, freedom of religion is a right for all Americans.

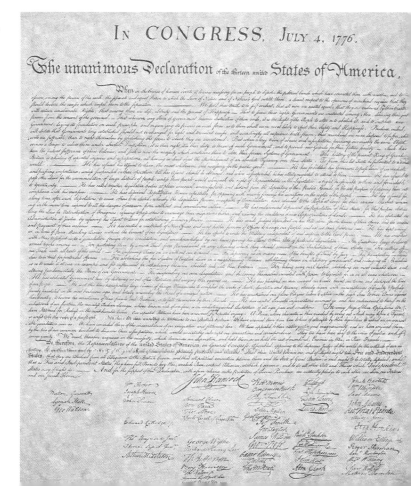

A copy of the Declaration of Independence

The Making of the 4th United States President

1751
Born March 16 in Port Conway, VA

1762
Enters Donald Robertson's School

1767
Tutored at home by Thomas Martin, a clergyman

1771
Graduates from College of New Jersey (Princeton)

1786
Elected to the Virginia Assembly

1787
Attends Constitutional Convention in Philadelphia

1788
Elected to the House of Representatives

1794
Marries Dolley Payne Todd in September

1808
Elected 4th president of the U.S.

1812
War of 1812—Madison is re-elected president

1814
English soldiers burn down the White House

1815
War of 1812 ends

1817
Returns home to Montpelier, VA—James Monroe becomes president

PRESIDENTIAL YEARS

James Madison

"The public good, the real welfare of the great body of the people, is the supreme object to be pursued..."

1774

Becomes a member of the County Committee for Public Safety

1776

Becomes a member of the Virginia Convention—works on the Virginia Bill of Rights and the Virginia Constitution

1779

Elected to the Continental Congress

Historical Highlights
during Madison Administration

Louisiana admitted as a state (1812)
Indiana admitted as a state (1816)

War of 1812

Washington, D.C., burned by the British

Hartford Convention

1801

Appointed secretary of state

1803

Louisiana Purchase

1829

Takes part in the Virginia Constitutional Convention

1833

Opposes slavery—becomes president of American Colonization Society

1836

Dies on June 28, at the age of 85

We the People

*I*n the early 1780s, James Madison served in the Second Continental **Congress**, the group who met in Philadelphia to decide laws for the whole country. James thought the states should pay **taxes** to support the country. But the states fought with each other over many things. They wanted to keep their money for themselves, not give it to the country to share with other states.

People were afraid a strong government would act like a king. They did not want that! How could the U.S. be strong enough to take care of its people, but not so strong that it might hurt them? This was the question on people's minds.

By 1787, the leaders of the new United States saw that their new country was in trouble. They did not have money or a strong army. They wanted to hold another **convention** to discuss new rules for the country. But the states were so angry that they did not even want to talk to each other!

That year there was a terrible riot in Massachusetts called Shays's Rebellion. The new U.S. government was so weak it could not even stop this riot. This scared everybody. Now everyone knew there had to be a Constitutional **Convention** to save the country.

James Madison went to the convention. He wrote plans for a stronger U.S. government. The plans included three parts, or **branches**, to the government (the executive, the judicial, and the legislative). Each part balanced the other parts.

The ideas became part of a paper explaining new rules for the United States. This paper is the United States **Constitution**. "We the people" are its famous first words. And James Madison still is remembered as the Father of the Constitution.

The U.S. Constitution

Wise Leadership

*I*n 1788, James Madison was elected to serve in the House of Representatives. This group was part of the new system described in the **Constitution**. As a member of the House, James argued for and won a new **tax** law. Now the new United States government had a way to make money.

James Madison also helped write another important paper called the Bill of Rights. This paper explains 10 rights that belong to every American. Freedom of religion is one of these rights.

In 1794, James married a widow named Dolley Payne Todd. James was 43, and most people thought he would never marry. He was quiet, worked hard, and did not have many friends. But Dolley liked to laugh and go to parties. She helped James feel happier around other people.

Also in 1794, John Adams was elected the second president of the United States. John belonged to a party called the Federalists. James and his good friend Thomas

First Lady Dolley Madison in her later years

Jefferson were a part of the Republican party. These were the first **political parties** in the United States.

The Republicans and the Federalists fought about everything! When John Adams, a Federalist, was elected, James Madison knew his ideas would not be liked. So he went home to Virginia.

But in 1800, Thomas Jefferson was elected the third president of the United States. He asked James Madison to be his secretary of state. The secretary of state meets with leaders from other countries to discuss important things like war, peace, trading, and shipping.

In 1803, James helped Thomas buy all the land between the Mississippi River and the Rocky Mountains. The land belonged to France, but because of the Napoleonic Wars, France was at war with England. So France didn't have the time, money, or energy to take care of this land. Thomas Jefferson bought it for a very low price. This was called the Louisiana Purchase.

The war between England and France dragged on. The United States stayed **neutral**.

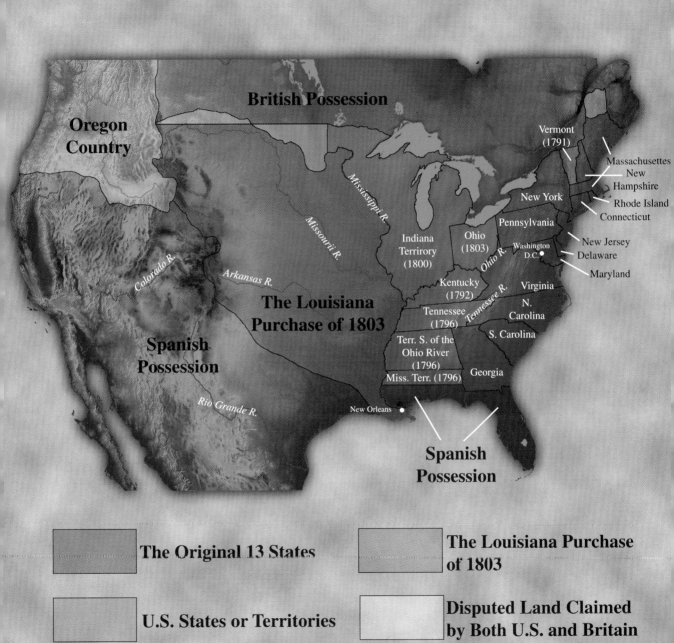

Oregon Country

British Possession

Spanish Possession

The Louisiana Purchase of 1803

Spanish Possession

Vermont (1791)

Massachusettes
New Hampshire
Rhode Island
Connecticut
New York
Pennsylvania
New Jersey
Delaware
Maryland

Indiana Terrirory (1800)

Ohio (1803)

Washington D.C.

Kentucky (1792)

Virginia

N. Carolina

Tennessee (1796)

S. Carolina

Terr. S. of the Ohio River (1796)

Miss. Terr. (1796)

Georgia

New Orleans

Mississippi R.

Missourii R.

Colorado R.

Arkansas R.

Ohio R.

Tennessee R.

Rio Grande R.

The Original 13 States

The Louisiana Purchase of 1803

U.S. States or Territories

Disputed Land Claimed by Both U.S. and Britain

President Madison

*I*n 1808, the Republicans chose Madison to run for president, and in November, he was elected the fourth president of the United States. In March 1809, he and Dolley moved to their new home in the new capital city, Washington, D.C.

President Madison faced many troubles. France and England were still at war. At sea, both countries attacked U.S. ships to get more men and money for their sides.

James tried to keep the U.S. **neutral**. He tried to make trade deals with France and England to stop the attacks.

The Federalists and Republicans were at war, too—with each other! Many Federalist leaders called James Madison terrible names, accused him of things, and would not do as he asked. At one point, some Federalists from the northeastern states even plotted to secede from, or pull out of, the United States and form their own country.

James's friends were surprised that he did not punish these people for this crime, called **treason**. But James believed strongly in freedom for all people to speak their minds, even when they do not agree with their president.

In 1812, James was elected to a second term as president. The U.S. was in a war with England. Today this war is called the War of 1812. Many U.S. generals were weak, and many leaders who did not like James continued to work against him in many ways.

One night, English soldiers came to Washington, D.C. Fearing the worst, Dolley Madison cut a famous picture of President George Washington out of its frame and carried it to safety. Others carried away the **Declaration of Independence** and other important papers. Soon English soldiers burned down almost every building in the city!

Finally, the war turned around for the U.S. New generals like Andrew Jackson won important battles. On December 24th, 1814, a peace treaty was signed. By 1815, the war was finally over.

Better Times

*B*y the end of the War of 1812, people were angry with the Federalist party for attacking the president. So the Federalist party faded away and soon died out. Now the people who worked with James Madison were his friends. The fighting was truly over!

Laws were passed to help keep the U.S. Army and Navy strong. With the end of the war, it was safe for countries to trade on the seas again. The United States made money selling goods to other countries.

Before the war, Dolley Madison had many parties in the White House. After the White House was burned down by English soldiers, the Madisons lived in smaller houses. The White House was rebuilt, but not for many years.

In November 1816, James Madison's friend, James Monroe, was elected the fifth president of the Unitcd States. In 1817, James and Dolley Madison returned to Montpelier.

At home, many friends visited the Madisons, and they held many parties. James rode his horse through his plantation. He helped **advise** other leaders about Virginia laws. And now he had more time than ever to read the books he loved!

On June 28, 1836, at age 85, James Madison died quietly. Dolley moved back to Washington, D.C. She died in 1849.

James Madison

The Great Little Madison

•Soon after Dolley Payne Todd met James Madison, she wrote about him in a letter to a friend. She called him "the great little Madison."

•Dolley Madison was one of the most popular first ladies of all time. People liked her because she liked to laugh, was strong and pretty, and was kind to everybody—even people she didn't like.

•James Madison's father called him "Jemmie" as a boy, and the nickname stuck. Later, when the English burned down the White House in the War of 1812, the English general raised his glass and drank a toast to "Jemmie."

•The inaugural ball is a fancy party held in the White House every time a new president is elected and moves in. The first inaugural ball ever held was for James and Dolley Madison, in March 1809.

•James Madison was the last living man of the Founding Fathers, the group of men who signed the **Declaration of Independence** and helped create the United States of America.

The signing of the Declaration of Independence, 1776

Glossary

Advise—to help a person decide things.

Branches—three main groupings in the United States government system; they are the executive branch, the judicial branch, and the legislative branch, which includes the House of Representatives and the Senate; James Madison planned and wrote much of what became this system today.

Congress—one group of people in the United States government; the Congress helps decide laws, and members of Congress are elected by U.S. citizens.

Constitution—important rules written down on a piece of paper that describes freedom and rights for Americans.

Convention—a big meeting.

Declaration of Independence—an important paper that said the English colonies wanted to be free and start their own government.

Negotiate—to talk with other leaders about peace and freedom.

Neutral—to be on neither one side nor the other; not taking sides.

Party—a group of people organized to gain political power.

Politics—the process of making laws and running a government.

Retire—to give up an office or job.

Seizure—the strong squeezing action or loss of muscle control of a person's body, sometimes caused by heart diseases or epilepsy.

Taxes—extra fees paid to the government.

Treason—a crime that hurts the safety of a whole country; people found guilty of treason were often killed as punishment.

Tutor—a teacher who teaches one or only a few students.

Internet Sites

Welcome to the White House
www.whitehouse.gov

Visit the official Web site of the White House. There is an introduction from the United State's current president. Also included is extensive biographies of each president, White House history information, art in the White House, First Ladies, and First Families. Visit the section titled: The White House for Kids, where kids can become more active in the government of the United States.

Presidents of the United States – Potus
www.ipl.org/ref/POTUS/

This excellent Web site has background information and biographies on each president. Also included are results of every presidential election, cabinet members, presidency highlights, and some fun facts on each of the presidents. Links to historical documents, audio and video files, and other presidential sites are also included to enrich this site.

The James Madison Museum
www.jamesmadisonmuseum.org/

Visit the James Madison Museum Web site. Included in this site are photos, special exhibits, excellent links to other James Madison Web sites, and much more.

These sites are subject to change. Go to your favorite search engine and type in United States presidents for more sites.

Pass It On

History Enthusiasts: educate readers around the country by passing on information you've learned about presidents or other important people who've changed history. Share your little-known facts and interesting stories. We want to hear from you!

To get posted on the ABDO Publishing Company Web site, E-mail us at "History@abdopub.com"
Visit the ABDO Publishing Company Web site at www.abdopub.com

Index